Behind the Curtain

by   Kay Macaulife

KENYON – DEANE LTD.

LONDON

ACTING FEES FOR PERFORMANCES OVERSEAS

Apply to : **South Africa:** Mello House, PO Box 236, Sea Point 8060, Capetown. **Kenya:** National Theatre, PO Box 452, Nairobi. **Southern Rhodesia:** Association of Rhodesian Theatrical Soc., PO Box 2701, Salisbury. **Australia:** Will Andrade, 275c Pitt Street, Sydney, NSW, Australia 2000. **New Zealand:** Play Bureau, Box 3611, Wellington. **Canada & U.S.A.:** Walter H. Baker Co., Boston. **Holland:** International Bureau, Vondelstraat 102, Amsterdam.

ISBN No. 0 7155 0378 2

Copyright Kay Macaulife 1983.

Printed in England by Kenyon-Deane Ltd.

CAST:

E L L E N	Mary Tudor (aged 42)
A N G E L A :	A Writer
B E T T Y :	Assistant Stage Manager
R U T H :	Elizabeth Tudor (aged 29)
P H Y L L I S :	Wardrobe Mistress

SCENE:

A Dressing Room in a Village Hall, somewhere in England. There is a door, centre back. Left and Right are two plain wooden chairs, facing two tables, which have mirrors on them, also jars and bottles of make-up and a script.

On table Right (Ellen's) is a vacuum flask and a down-turned glass.

On table Left (Ruth's) is a vacuum flask with a cup cover. On each table a bunch of roses with card attached.

Around the walls are strings and shoulder-hangers. One holds modern clothes (Ruth's) and another a dress for Mary Tudor (Ellen's); other period costumes could hang about the room if available. If desired there could be a screen.

The CAST are members of an Amateur Dramatic Society. The age of the Cast is immaterial, but BETTY could be a younger member.

TIME:

The present — evening.

PROPERTIES REQUIRED:

Pencil and list	BETTY.
Tray with two wine goblets	PHYLLIS.

PERIOD COSTUMES REQUIRED:

QUEEN MARY	ELLEN
PRINCESS ELIZABETH	RUTH
LADY — IN — WAITING	BETTY

Behind the Curtain

The Curtain rises on an empty stage. Ellen opens the door and hesitates as though unwilling to enter. She is good-looking and smartly dressed, but obviously very tense. She sees the roses on her table, smiles and crosses to them. She takes up and reads the card. In the act of removing her coat she turns to face the second table, her smile fades and she crosses slowly, her hands hover over the roses. There is a knock at the door, and Ellen turns quickly away.

ELLEN: Come in!

ANGELA: *(looks in. She is dressed in practical clothes, suitable for a dress rehearsal)* May I? .... May I, really? .... *(she enters)* Well, if you're sure I'm not disturbing you .. .. Oh, Ellen, how lovely you look — but then you always do.

ELLEN: I'm quite sure I don't! But, thanks all the same. One of the few privileges I've managed to wrest from our stony-hearted Producer is to make up at home in peace. He knows I'll arrive at the right place, at the right time, and with the right face on.

ANGELA: Prepared to put up a splendid performance as usual.

ELLEN: Goodness, Angela, are you determined to ruin the Show? Such heedless optimism is tempting the Gods!

ANGELA: *(quietly)* They've done their worst already, I hope, to me and to you, and to my poor little play.

ELLEN: You've had to wait a long time for your first production. I hope you won't be disappointed.

1

ANGELA: I'm sure I shan't You're wonderful as Mary Tudor,
          Ellen, really wonderful.

ELLEN: Well, you've written a marvellous part for me. It's got
          everything an actress could wish for.

ANGELA: *(fingering script on Ellen's table)* I've always wanted
          to write about her. She was such a complex character, and
          she had so much to contend with. All her life she was sur-
          rounded with enemies; her throne, and her very life, threat-
          ened by the young half sister she both loved and feared.
          No wonder she went mad in the end.

ELLEN: She won't be the only one to go mad! Hugh will be rav-
          ing if I'm not dressed in time, you know what a stickler for
          punctuality he is.

ANGELA: Oh, do let me help you. May I?

ELLEN: Please do, if you'd like to. *(with Angela's assistance
          Ellen gets into her costume.   Ellen should be dressed for
          the rehearsal scene)* These period costumes are the very
          devil to get into. How women conducted all those love
          affairs in them I can't imagine, and they seem to do nothing
          else!

ANGELA: Love mattered more when it was dangerous. Romance
          was often a matter of life and death in Tudor times. People
          don't feel so deeply now, there's no romance in modern living.

ELLEN: Nonsense, Angela, there's plenty of romance if you look
          for it, people feel just as deeply.   Look at mixed marriages,
          and all those passionate teenage elopements, why don't you
          write about those?

ANGELA: They don't appeal to me as a writer and, anyway, I
          never meet people like that. The ones I know are like the
          members of this Society, living quiet respectable lives, and
          using acting as an outlet for their emotions, on the stage they
          feel uninhibited . . . .

ELLEN: Do you really imagine anyone can feel uninhibited in this
          lot? Why on earth don't you stick to classical greek or

roman togas. I'd hate to run for a bus in this skirt, and as for driving a car .... *(there is a pause, instinctively they glance at the other table)* ... Where's Ruth?

ANGELA: I haven't seen her. I'd like to wish her luck, this rehearsal is sure to be a bit of an ordeal for her.

ELLEN: *(briskly)* Nonsense. That's what understudies are for — to be ready to go on in the event of an accident. All understudies long for a chance and this is Ruth's She ought to be on top of the world.

ANGELA: How could she be, Ellen? In the circumstances.

ELLEN: In what circumstances?

ANGELA: Well, this wasn't an ordinary accident, was it? If Pat hadn't died as she did, in the middle of a dress rehearsal ....

ELLEN: You mean it was inconsiderate of her to dash out of the theatre, jump into her car and crash it. So upsetting for Ruth?

ANGELA: Ellen dear, don't you think — for all our sakes — it would be better to forget it? I mean, not really *forget* it, of course — but, not to refer to it? It was a dreadful shock to us all, worse for you — because you were such friends, but ....

ELLEN: It's because we were friends, real friends,that I can't accept the Coroner's verdict. Pat didn't drink that night, she told me so herself, and I believe her, and they found alcohol in her body. How did it get there? I want to know the truth, and I mean to find it. If Ruth's feelings or anyone else's, get hurt in the process, that's too bad.

ANGELA: But what are you trying to prove? It's perfectly obvious what happened, surely?

ELLEN: Not to me it isn't. I knew Pat, and Pat knew her weakness and she guarded against it in every way she could. I just do not believe that she got stewed to the eyebrows in the middle of a dress rehearsal, with a glorious part to play and the man she loved sitting out there watching her. I don't believe it,

3

I tell you.

ANGELA: But, Ellen, what is the alternative? Do you seriously imagine anyone in this Society would give Pat knock-out drops in order to drive her out of the theatre to her death?

ELLEN: No, Of course not. I'm not looking for a murderer, only for the truth. I've got to find it. Pat wasn't a very happy person, her marriage was on the rocks, and she hadn't many friends. This Society, the people in it, and her acting meant everything to her. She would never let us down, and it was because she realised that we thought she had, that she was so upset. When she came back to the dressing room she was bewildered, completely bewildered. I asked her what had happened, and she said: "Hugh says I'm drunk, and I'm not, Ellen, I swear I'm not. You must tell him. I'm ill, I must be ill, but I'm not drunk. Tell him, Ellen." I didn't want to leave her, but she was so distressed and so insistent that I went . . . . when I came back her costume was in a heap on the floor, and she'd gone . . . . She'd jumped into her car and driven off . . . . Her mind wasn't working properly, or she would never have done that . . . . don't you see? She didn't reallise the risk she was taking, because she didn't realise that she was drunk.

ANGELA: I think that's perfactly understandable. These costumes are very heavy, and the stage gets terribly hot under the lights. If she only took a small amount . . . .

ELLEN: She couldn't have done.

ANGELA: But how can you know?

ELLEN: Because she had nothing to take. There was no bottle of any kind in the car when they . . . when they found her. I packed her things up myself that night; there was nothing here, nothing but her usual flask of coffee.

ANGELA: (glances at the flask on Ruth's table) And . . . ?

ELLEN: It was untouched.

ANGELA: But, that doesn't *prove* anything, Ellen, don't you see . . ?

4

BETTY: *(knocks and enters hastily. She is in slacks and an old
            jumper. She carries a list and there is a pencil behind her ear.*
            If you want to check your props, Ellen, they're all together
            on the card table nearest to the stage; don't lean on it, it's
            only got three legs. And do be careful of your sceptre;the
            ball on the top fell off again, so do remember to keep it up-
            right until the glue's had time to dry. And Hugh says re-
            member to sit well back on your throne, it still wobbles a
            bit.

ELLEN: Thank you Betty dear. After such encouraging news I
            will endeavour to go through my part with queenly dignity,
            while rocking like a ship at sea, and with bits of my regalia
            flying off in all directions.

BETTY: Just thought you'd like to know the worst .... Now,
            I've only got the wine to do before I get dressed ....
            Having to play Ruth's part as well as doing the props is
            driving me mad, if only ....

ANGELA: *(hastily)* Where is Ruth?

BETTY: Having her face done, and then Hugh wants to go through
            her big scene before we start rehearsal. She's in a terrible
            state, and I don't wonder. It must be awful to take over a
            huge part like Elizabeth after, well ....

ELLEN: Nonsense, Betty. This is her chance, and it's up to her
            to use it — no matter how it came her way, that's the only
            way to look at it.

BETTY: Well, it's not the way I look at it! Just because Ruth has
            to play Elizabeth I'm landed with the Lady-in-Waiting, and
            the only chance it will give me is to make a damned fool of
            myself. I shall either go on with a list in my hand, and a
            pencil behind my ear, or miss an entrance while I try to cope
            backstage. All I ask is to get that ghastly costume off, and
            get on with my real job.

ANGELA: You haven't actually got it on yet, Betty, and this is a
            dress rehearsal.

BETTY: Heavens! Yes! Hugh will eat me if I'm late. Good luck,

5

Ellen, you're sure to be marvellous, you always are. You terrify me in the mad scene — you know, when you go round the bend because you're not pregnant when you think you are. You're so natural.

ELLEN: Well, thank you for the — er — compliment, dear.

BETTY: Mary must have been nuts to mind so much. You'd think she'd be thankful to get out of it at her age.

ANGELA: The birth of an heir was a matter of great importance both to her, and to the state.

ELLEN: And to us, too — if Mary had had a child there might have been no Elizabethan Age — no tobacco and no potatoes — think of that! Anyone care for a cigarette? *(the cast could smoke or not as desired)*

BETTY: Well, it didn't bother her husband much anyway. He couldn't have cared less. Men get the best of it everytime, if you ask me, you never hear of them going round the bend because they're not fathers after all, and yet they behave as if it's all their own work when . . . .

Ruth enters. She is in full Elizabethan costume, with a make-up wrapper over her shoulders. She is followed by Phyllis, in a nylon overall, a tape measure round her neck and a pin-cushion strapped to her wrist. Ruth is very keyed up and nervous.

RUTH: Hallo, everybody.

ANGELA: Hallo, dear.

ELLEN: *(coldly)* Good evening.

BETTY: *(moving to door)* Hallo and Goodbye, Ruth. See you later, when I am transformed into a member of the Nobility, forsooth!

RUTH: That'll be the day! *(she moves to her table)* Roses! From Hugh, of course. *(she reads card, and laughs)* Flatterer! Your husband is a clever man, Phyllis. Presenting us with flowers before a dress rehearsal, so he can feel free to tear us to pieces afterwards. *(she removes wrap)*

6

PHYLLIS: *(her whole attention on costume)* Stand still a minute, dear. I want to see that hem.

ELLEN: And why shouldn't he? He's a Producer, and a damn good one, and what he gets out of this ordinary little group of amateurs is incredible. You can't make an omelette without breaking eggs.

RUTH: You can't get blood out of a stone, either. I wish he'd stop trying to work miracles with me. I've longed — I've almost prayed — for the chance to play Elizabeth, and now I've got it, and I can't do it, I can't.

ELLEN: Really? I wonder why?

RUTH: Because your precious Producer is trying to turn me into another Pat, and I'm not, I'm not. I *could* play Elizabeth, I know I could, but in my own way. She was such a fascinating character, clever as a fox in evading danger; ruthless in the way she used her friends and lovers; fighting every inch of the way to avoid danger and death, and in the face of impossible odds somehow getting her own way.

ELLEN: You feel type cast, perhaps?

RUTH: Just what do you mean by that, Ellen?

PHYLLIS: Do stand still, Ruth, I don't think that skirt is quite even, Angela, do you?

ANGELA: It looks lovely, Phyllis, really lovely. I think it's amazing how you've done it in the time; it's just as good as — the other — and yet, quite different.

RUTH: Yes, I'm thankful for that, I would have hated . . . .

ELLEN: To wear the dress worn by a corpse, if that's what you mean, why not say so?

RUTH: You hate me, don't you, Ellen? You really hate me. But, why? We used to be friends. Pat's dead. O.K., I'm sorry, but it's not my fault.

ELLEN: Isn't it? *(Ruth stares at her)*

ANGELA: Well, of course not. If Pat hadn't got so drunk she

7

would never have rushed out of the theatre like that.

ELLEN: Pat did not get drunk, how dare you, Angela.

RUTH: But, my dear Ellen, the inquest proved that she did, that she had consumed . . . .

ELLEN: Pat did not drink anything alcoholic in this theatre. She never drank at a dress rehearsal, or during a show.

RUTH: *(not unkindly)* How do you know what she did before she got here, Ellen?

ELLEN: Because I dressed with her, in this room, and I would have known. I knew her so well — we were friends — *(her voice is unsteady, but she does not give way)*

PHYLLIS: Ellen, please don't say any more. You have a long and difficult part to get through, and so has Ruth. This production means a lot to us all, to Angela, the Charities we work for and to the Society. Can't we concentrate on making a success of it, all of us?

RUTH: Hear hear! For goodness sake let's pull together and make a go of it. *(to Ellen)* I'm not Pat, but I'll do my best, if you'll help me.

ELLEN: *(suddenly. There is no hint of softness in her voice or manner)* All right, I'll help you. Let's run through a scene together now. The one where I summon you to drink to my unborn child.

RUTH: *(surprised)* But — why that one? It's nearly the end of the play.

ELLEN: It won't take a minute, it's very short, and it will give Betty a chance to do a bit too.

RUTH: All right. Thank you Ellen. *(Phyllis moves to door)*

PHYLLIS: I'll fetch Betty.

ELLEN: Ask her to bring the goblets, will you? *(Phyllis exits)* Angela can prompt — you can use my script.

ANGELA: I don't need it, I know every word.

RUTH: Then you'd better play my part, for I'm sure I don't!

ANGELA: You know Ruth, perhaps I shouldn't say this, but I do honestly think that you are quite as good as Pat in this part. Even better, in some ways.

RUTH: *(genuinely delighted)* Thank you, Angela, I'm so glad you think so. It is a difficult part, but I love playing it, and I'm more anxious than ever not to let the Society down.

Voices are heard off. Betty, in a period skirt and her own old jumper comes in with a period bodice over her arm. She is followed by Phyllis carrying a tray containing two wine goblets.

PHYLLIS: You should be dressed by now, Betty.

BETTY: But I haven't made the wine yet! And anyway, I can't breathe in that bodice, I just can't breathe! Something seems to be caught up somewhere, and it's agony! I shall open my mouth on the stage, and nothing will come, just nothing! Can't you loosen it, or something?

Phyllis puts tray on Ruth's table, takes bodice from Betty and moves to door.

PHYLLIS: I'll see to it while you rehearse. *(she exits)*

BETTY: Oh, thank you, Phyllis .... Where are you going from?

ELLEN: Ruth's entrance. *(she turns her chair to face Centre Front. Ruth and Betty move Down stage Left to an imagined entrance. Ellen sits, assuming a regal pose, but betraying great weariness.)*

BETTY: The scene I dread most! What with coping with those terribly wobbly goblets, and remembering to curtsey all the time, and walk backwards! My feet get tangled up in my skirt, and my hands feel like great pink hams on the end of my arms, and my tongue sticks to the roof of my mouth ....

RUTH: *(laughing)* She makes me wonder how I ever tackled the Lady-in-Waiting! It sounds much worse than playing Elizabeth. Are you ready?

BETTY: Yes, but you'll have to imagine the wine — it's not made yet. *(she curtseys)* When I curtsey my knees go off like pistons — do you think the audience will notice?

RUTH: They'll be so dumfounded by the quality of your perform-ance they'll be struck dumb, and deaf too, probably. Go on, announce me.

BETTY: *(takes a step or two forward towards Ellen and curtsies)* Your Majesty, the Princess Elizabeth.

RUTH: *(moves forward and makes deep curtsey, remaining down)* You sent for me, Your Majesty?

ELLEN: *(signals her to rise. Betty moves to behind Ellen's chair)* Yes — We sent for you — We have need of you. There is a task for you here, one that no other subject can fulfill.

RUTH: Any thing Your Majesty desires.

ELLEN: Can you not tell why We have brought you here? . . . . Now you are in Our presence . . . . Is it not plain enough? . . . . Look well, Elizabeth — what do you see?

RUTH: I see my Sovereign. The Quuen of England.

ELLEN: And — what more do you see? Speak!

RUTH: *(in a desperate manner)* I see the beloved sister with whom I shared my childhood. The sister who cared for me, and romped with me, who called me 'Bess' — and trusted me as I trusted her. Oh, Mary — Your Majesty — those far off days, when our brother reigned and we were both out of favour; those years of exile and poverty were bitter indeed, but sweetened by the hours we spent together. We were together in spirit in our shared adversity; I have not changed — why have you turned from me? Why cannot you trust me now, as you trusted me then?

ELLEN: Those days are gone — you have grown stubborn, unre-pentant in your denial of the true faith. You wish Us ill, you turn Our subjects from Us, you covet Our very Throne.

RUTH: Never, Madam, never! You cannot think so ill of me. Your Majesty has no truer subject — the plots that surround

10

Your Majesty are not of my making; if my name is taken it is without my knowledge — you must believe that it is so.

ELLEN: If We could but trust you — We are so alone, and in desperate need of comfort and support — the days drag by, and the nights are long and lonely . . . . .

RUTH: Then trust me, Your Majesty, let all be as it was when we were children, before the cares of State and the ambitions of others divided us. Take me into your confidence, let me share your burden.

ELLEN: How can I trust you? — You who would give your very soul to occupy the Throne, and yet — if you would but share Our faith — the faith — you so stubbornly reject

RUTH: My loyalty has not wavered through the long years of imprisonment. I have remained a loyal and true subject, but my faith — if Your Majesty could but persuade me — how gladly would I submit, but such conversion must come from the soul, not from the tongue. Would you have me perjure myself — how could you trust me then? Your Majesty, you are not well, you are in pain . . . .

ELLEN: You know I am with child?

RUTH: I have heard it is so, and I rejoice for Your Majesty.

ELLEN: You lie! How could *you* rejoice in the child who will prove the death of all your ambitions and your hopes? You, who would have seized Our Throne with the connivance of Our most hated enemies — You who will never have it now!

RUTH: I speak the truth, Your Majesty, every subject must rejoice in such good fortune!

ELLEN: Good fortune! If only it prove true — it must be so — but the time is so long delayed . . . . they said in June . . . then again, in July . . . . August is here and almost gone, and still I feel no movement.

RUTH: I have heard it said, Your Majesty, that the babe quietens before it s time is nigh.

11

ELLEN: Then you believe it?   Do not lie, Elizabeth, you must not
           lie to me — for the sake of all you hold most dear — do
           you believe that a child will be born?

RUTH: But Your Majesty, I am no physician, how could I deny
           what your Advisors must know so much more surely
           than I?

ELLEN: If we could trust their word — it seems as if they, too,
           are afraid — but a woman must know, she at least cannot
           be wrong, only a little patience, a little longer to endure
           . . . . see this ring, my marriage ring — kiss it, Elizabeth,
           kneel and kiss the ring, and swear your allegiance to the
           child.   Down on your knees.

RUTH: *(obeying, but defiant)* Why, gladly, Your Majesty, I will
           pledge my troth — to the Future Sovereign of England!

ELLEN: The Future Sovereign of England — Philip's child and
           mine!   If only Philip were here to support me —

RUTH: He will come soon enough, Madam, when he hears what
           all England waits to hear.

ELLEN: *(to Betty, who curtseys and goes to Ruth's table)* Fetch
           wine!   We will drink a toast together . . . . you will stay
           at my side and you shall be well watched — you can do no
           mischief here.

RUTH: But Your Majesty, if I may advise you — you must not
           disturb yourself, you have another to consider now.   You
           should have about you only those who soothe and comfort,
           it is my tragedy that my presence can never add to your
           tranquility.   For your sake, and the sake of the child, I beg
           Your Majesty to let me go.

ELLEN: No, Elizabeth, your place is here.   It is your duty to
           witness the birth of the Heir Apparent, for that you have
           been brought here, and for that you will remain until Our
           time has come.

           *Betty enters with goblets — she hands tray to Ellen, who
           takes a goblet then to Ruth.   She then returns to Ellen's*

side.

RUTH: *(with real sincerity)* Then I do sincerely pray that time will come quickly!

ELLEN: Let us drink to England and to all the future generations. May they be worthy of the heritage we built for them, and may they find peace and prosperity under their future Sovereign.

RUTH: Why, Your Majesty, no wish is dearer to my heart. I drink to the future Sovereign of England, and a long and glorious reign.

ELLEN: *(hands goblet to Betty)* I am sick and weary, I can drink no more.

RUTH: *(in triumph)* Have patience, just a little longer, Your Majesty, for from the bottom of my heart I do believe that your time has almost come!

She drains the goblet. There is a pause, then Betty takes goblet back to tray and Ellen rises.

BETTY: Was I alright?

RUTH: You were fine.

BETTY: Did I do it just as you did?

RUTH: Yes.

ELLEN: No!

ANGELA: Oh, but surely . . . .

ELLEN: *(to Ruth)* There was one difference — surely you haven't forgotten? When you handed me the goblet I spilt it — I didn't drink any.

BETTY: Oh, for goodness sake, don't remind me of that! I was trying to forget. I make enough mistakes of my own, without copying Ruth's.

ELLEN: If it was a mistake.

RUTH: Look here, just what are you getting at, Ellen?

ELLEN: Go and get dressed, Betty, the scene's finished.

BETTY: *(picking up tray and goblets)* Finished? It sounds to me as if it's only just started, only Angela didn't write this one. All right, I'm going. *(she exits)*

RUTH: Are you seriously suggesting that I spilt your wine on purpose, Ellen? Why on earth should I do that?

ELLEN: Pat was the only person to drink that wine — *what was in it?*

RUTH: You know perfectly well what was in it, the stuff we always use, that cherry cordial. It tastes pretty filthy, but it couldn't hurt anyone.

ELLEN: Not unless it had been tampered with.

RUTH. You mean — unless I had tampered with it. You're not serious — you can't be.

ELLEN: You wanted to play Elizabeth, didn't you? You said you'd do anything for the chance. Did you make Pat drunk on purpose, knowing how strict Hugh is about drinking in the theatre? Is that how you planned to get the part?

RUTH: I never heard such an absurd idea, how would I know that I'd get it, anyway? Hugh may be a disciplinarian, but even he would hesitate to throw anyone out of a leading part on the night before the show. And, what's more, I've just remembered something else — I didn't spill your wine, Ellen, you did.

ELLEN: You jogged my arm.

RUTH: And because of that, you cooked up this fantastic idea? All I can say is that you must be affected by Angela's play, it's the sort of typical Tudor mish-mash that might appeal to the characters we're playing, but not to me, nor to anyone else in this day and age.

ANGELA. I hope I could do better than that if I had to! It is an absurd idea, Ellen, you must see that.

ELLEN: Is it so absurd? When I know Pat did not drink that night, I know it, I tell you, *she did not drink.*

14

ANGELA: How can you be so sure, Ellen? We all know that Pat did drink, quite a lot at times. Perhaps she was emotionally upset over her part, and . . . .

RUTH: She was emotionally upset all right, but it wasn't over her part.

ELLEN: What do you mean?

RUTH: It wasn't what she drank that sent her to her death, it was Hugh's behaviour that did it. You didn't see what happened when he realised she wasn't fit to rehearse. He fairly tore into the poor girl, he left her without a shred of pride or self-confidence, just when she needed them most; it was a devastating performance, an particularly brutal when we all know that Pat was madly in love with him . . . .

Phyllis stands in the doorway.

Phyllis! I didn't see you, I'm sorry, I didn't mean . . . .

PHYLLIS: *(quietly)* Hugh's almost ready to start the rehearsal, Ruth, he wants to run through your big scene first.

RUTH: *(furiously)* That's all I needed! I shall make a complete hash of it — and it's all your fault. You're all right, Jack, aren't you? Your technique and vast professional experience will carry you through hell and high water, once you get on the stage. But you might remember that the rest of us are only poor struggling amateurs, and give us a chance to get on with the Show.

ANGELA: *(urging Ruth to door)* Come along Ruth, don't keep Hugh waiting.

RUTH: Pat's dead, Ellen, and nothing you can do will bring her back, so why not accept the fact, and shut up about it until the Show is over. *(to Angela)* All right, I'm going. *(she exits)*

ANGELA: *(following her off)* But you mustn't upset yourself, Ruth . . . .

PHYLLIS: I've never seen Ruth so nervous, I do hope she'll be alright. *(she sits wearily)* We do want this Production to

15

be a success, it's a very ambitious one.

ELLEN: It won't be your fault if it fails. You and Hugh have worked enough — you always do. Between us we've built this little Dramatic Society into something we can be proud of, and I'm proud of it, too. I want Angela's play to be a success, but it's not a matter of life and death, is it? Other things are more important . . . .

PHYLLIS: No, not a matter of life and death — but at least it's not too late to achieve something, to affect the result. You can't alter the past, Ellen, why not accept the facts, and try to forget?

ELLEN: I can't forget, and it's not too late, it's never too late to learn the truth . . . . I can't alter what happened, but I can't accept it either. Don't you see, Phyllis, this is my chance. Here we are, in the same place, running through the same rehearsal, only with an understudy instead of Pat. Why did it happen? Why? Why?

PHYLLIS: I think I know why it happened, what made Pat act as she did.

ELLEN: You know? What is it, Phyllis, you must tell me. I've got to know the truth.

PHYLLIS: I didn't mean to tell anyone — if I confide in you, you must promise to respect my confidence.

ELLEN: Of course I will. And I'll do everything I can to make the Show a success, but I must know what happened.

PHYLLIS: Pat was under a great strain that night, she was in love with Hugh — that was obvious to everyone. And all these weeks he'd lavished attention on her, flattered her outrageously, just to bring out everything she could give — for the sake of the production. The last production of the season, it would all be over when the curtain fell for the last time. She knew his interest in her would die as soon as she'd given the performance he'd coaxed and bullied out of her, and she couldn't face it. So she wrote to him, begg-

16

ing him not to break off their friendship, to continue to see her, begging for more than he could give . . . .

ELLEN: Did Hugh tell you this?

PHYLLIS: No, he didn't know, Ellen, no one knew. You see, she never delivered the letter. Perhaps she never would have done; perhaps it was just an outlet for her emotions, an expression of the feeling she couldn't give vent to in any other way.

ELLEN: But how do you know this?

PHYLLIS: I found the letter, it was in the posket of her costume, do you want to read it?

ELLEN: No . . . . No.

PHYLLIS: I didn't find it until after the inquest and, even if I had, what difference would it have made? It didn't alter anything, but it explains why Pat was so desperate, so unhappy — don't you see, Ellen?

ELLEN: You want me to believe that she tried to drown her sorrows? It doesn't make sense. Pat was a fighter, and she had everything to gain by making a success of her part. And, she would have done, she would have made Hugh proud of her, don't you see? That's what she meant to do, to prove to him that she was capable of doing all he asked, and then — then gamble everything on her pride.

PHYLLIS: She would have lost, no woman would ever win Hugh that way.

ELLEN: You seem very sure, Phyllis. Amateur Dramatics can prove a dangerous hobby. Working with people, releasing their inhibitions, rousing their emotions — it's like playing with fire. Someone is bound to get burnt in the end. Don't you think that one day it might be Hugh?

PHYLLIS: No, never. I know him too well People are like puppets to him, there to be worked on, and used for his beloved theatre. He's no time for real emotions when he's producing, they only get in his way. He's a dedicated professional,

17

like you, Ellen, you and Hugh will both be professionals all your lives, in spite of the fact that you no longer work in the theatre.

ELLEN: That's why we understand each other so well. We've both chosen safety and security, but we can't resist the lure of the footlights altogether! We can laugh now at our failures, and live over our triumphs, and try to build something worth while in our safe little playground .... I wouldn't change my life or risk my security, I've got a good home and a loving husband and family, but I enjoy my little triumphs and my local fame.

PHYLLIS: And so does Hugh! I don't care for the theatrical side of it all, the mannerisms and the petty jealousies, but it is exciting to watch so many people and so many different talents combining together to achieve a common purpose. If the play is a success I feel all the effort is worth while, and I'm proud of being part of it, and if it isn't — well Hugh gave up his career in the theatre for me, the least I can do is to help him with the one thing he really cares about — the theatre. I don't mind watching other women wearing the dresses I've created, I don't mind seeing them accept the bunches of roses, as long as I've a garden to grow them in, and the whole long lovely summer to share it with Hugh. He's a different person when he's not working on a production, so gentle — so considerate —

Ruth rushes in, she flings her roses to the ground and starts tugging at her costume. Angela follows and hovers anxiously. Phyllis rises, picks up the flowers and returns them to the table.

RUTH: He's inhuman! He's cruel! I won't go on. I'm no good in the part, and never will be! I'm not going through with it.

PHYLLIS: *(moving to door, to Ellen)* I've kept my part of the bargain, now it's up to you. *(she exits)*

RUTH: *(to Angela)* Leave me alone, Angela, and don't you dare tell me how brilliant I was — don't you dare!

ANGELA: A bad dress rehearsal —

RUTH: We all know tnat one, it's as phony as the one about the understudy stealing the show, they're equally idiotic, theatrical fairy stories.

ELLEN: Understudies have stolen the show before now, but only when they happened to have guts and talent — you appear to have neither.

RUTH: You've already made your opinion of me quite clear, haven't you? Well, now I'll give you the satisfaction of proving you right. By walking out.

ELLEN: *(giving her a shake and pushing her into her chair)* Now sit down and take a few deep breaths, you've got a show to do, remember.

RUTH: Oh no, not me, not any more.

ELLEN: Stop talking nonsense and pull yourself together.

RUTH: Why should I? I'm not a professional actress, you know, I'm not getting paid, why should I put up with insults?

ELLEN: Because you're an actress, aren't you? You've got a wonderful part, and a producer who's trying to help you to play it. Do you expect it to be easy? Do you want to be part of a tatty little amateur production, or one of a team working under a competent producer to create something really worth while, something we can all be proud of.?

RUTH: You're a fine one to talk about team work, I must say, after the way you went for me.

ELLEN: I don't want the Show to suffer, that won't help. You can play Elizabeth if you put out of your mind that you're only second choice for the part. That's what's holding you back, forget it, you're darn lucky to have the chance however it came your way, any actress would go down on her knees to be in your shoes.

ANGELA: Oh thank you, Ellen.

ELLEN: I'll help you all I can. We'll do it together. And, I'm sorry for what I said, I was wrong — about you.

RUTH: Think nothing of it. *(she rises and straightens her costume)* I've been a wee bit on edge myself these last few weeks .... if only these costumes weren't so heavy. *(she sits)*

ANGELA: *(fussing over her)* Sit down and rest, dear, that's right. You mustn't get over-tired.

ELLEN: Have a drink and cool off a bit.

RUTH: *(picking up flask and then replacing it)* I've only brought coffee, can't think why — I've gone right off it lately. What I'd really like is a long cool drink of water.

ANGELA: That's the one thing you can't have in this Hall. We don't want you down with typhoid!

ELLEN: *(pouring a glass from her flask)* Here — have orange juice instead.

RUTH: *(accepting it)* Thanks — what, no gin?

ELLEN: That's what Pat used to say. She always teased me about my tipple. She was glad enough of a glass at dress rehearsal — she found the costumes just as heavy as you do. *(Ruth sits sipping her drink.)*

BETTY: *(runs in, now wearing her period costume)* I say, are you all right? You did give me a scare, rushing off like that, well — not really, of course. Hugh did go for you, didn't he? Hope he doesn't tear into me like that, still, we artistes have to suffer for our art, don't we? *(she curtseys)*

ELLEN: You seem very cool and collected all of a sudden. What's happened to the tangled feet and ham-like hands?

BETTY: *(walking round as she speaks)* Oh, it's different when you're properly dressed for the part. I wish I'd lived in Tudor times, when men were men and women were always being wronged — I bet they adored it. You know, I think I'll come on the acting side next year.

ANGELA: If you do, I'll write a part specially for you, Betty.

20

BETTY: Thanks very much, but I'd better see how I get on with this one first. We're not started yet though. I say Ruth, you'd better hurry — he's in no mood to be kept waiting.

RUTH: What's he waiting for?

BETTY: You.

RUTH: *Me?*

BETTY: Oh, didn't I tell you? He wants to do your bit again.

RUTH: *(jumping up)* Good heavens, why on earth didn't you say so? He'll be — here, take this — *(she hands glass to Ellen, then sways and sits again)* Oh — oh dear!

ANGELA: What is it? What's the matter?

RUTH: Nothing. I — I feel a bit giddy, that's all.

ELLEN: *(to herself, staring at the glass in her hand)* Oh no! No!

ANGELA: Put your head down and sit quietly, dear. *(to Betty)* Tell Hugh Ruth won't be long, Betty, ask him to wait.

BETTY: Ask him to — ? Oh well, he can't eat me — can he? *(she exits)*

ELLEN: *(holding glass out to Angela)* Angela, this orange juice —

ANGELA: Never mind that now, Ellen.

ELLEN: But I gave Pat a glass — that night —

ANGELA: Very kind of you. *(to Ruth)* How do you feel?

RUTH: Better. It's nothing really, I'm all right. Really I am. Just a bit giddy, that's all.

ANGELA: Have you felt like this before?

RUTH: Yes, just once or twice. I've been off my food a bit just lately. Perhaps I've got a chill.

ANGELA: Did you have any breakfast this morning?

RUTH: No, as a matter of fact, I've rather gone off that too.

ANGELA: How long have you been like this — off your food I mean?

RUTH: About a month, I suppose. Since Pat — since I've been

working on the part. Don't worry, I won't let you down, Angela. I'm not ill.

ANGELA: No, I don't think you are.

ELLEN: I can't understand it; you were all right until you had that drink, but I mixed it myself, at home. What does it mean?

ANGELA: I think I know what it means. Can't you guess, Ellen? Why should she suddenly turn faint like that? A healthy woman like Ruth.

ELLEN: You mean she's drunk?

ANGELA: Of course she's not drunk! She's pregnant!

RUTH: Preg — ?

ELLEN: *(sitting)* Oh, thank God!

ANGELA: Well, aren't you? Didn't you go off breakfast when your babies were coming, Ellen?

ELLEN: Yes, I did.

ANGELA: And I couldn't face coffee for weeks . . . . Have you thought of that possibility, Ruth?

RUTH: No . . . . I haven't . . . . I've been so occupied with the play and — we've waited so long, and almost given up hope . . . . Angela! I believe you may be right. I really believe you may be right . . . . Why ever didn't I think of it? Oh, wouldn't it be wonderful!

ANGELA: A new member of the Society! Make sure it's a boy, won't you? We're always short of men.

PHYLLIS: *(enters)* Ruth, are you alright?

RUTH: All right? I'm fine, just fine.

PHYLLIS: Are you sure? Hugh says he'll leave that scene if you'd rather, and start the rehearsal.

RUTH: *(rising)* Certainly not! I'm just in the mood to give the performance of my life. Hugh will be on his knees to me to play all the leads next year but I may not be available — too

22

busy with my own production.

BETTY: *(runs on)* I say, Ruth, Hugh says — *(there is a crash off-stage and a voice calls "Betty! Betty!)* Oh no! Not again! If it's happened again I'll die! I'll just die!

ELLEN: Don't tell me, let me guess — my Throne has gone through the floor at last.

BETTY: No, I expect it's that filthy raspberry cordial gone again. You'll have nothing to drink your toast with —

RUTH: Oh yes, we will. We'll drink it in champagne — well, on the last night, anyway! "To the future generation — may they find peace and prosperity under their future Sovereign!" Champagne or nothing!

BETTY: Well, tonight it's nothing! *(she exits)*

PHYLLIS: Don't keep Hugh waiting, Ruth!

RUTH: I'm on my way.

ELLEN: Good luck, Ruth!

RUTH: Thanks. *(she exits with Phyllis)*

ELLEN: There goes another promising actress lost to us for ever, probably!

ANGELA: Whatever made you think she was drunk?

ELLEN: It was so strange. I'd given Pat a drink of orange juice, just before she went on, and —

ANGELA: You're still convinced that she didn't take anything, aren't you, Ellen?

ELLEN: I told you she had nothing to take.

ANGELA: And I told you that proved nothing. Have you forgotten Hugh's little weakness? He's strict enough with his cast, but he's not above indulging himself when things don't go well. You can bet he had a bottle tucked away somewhere, vodka probably. She could have found that.

ELLEN: Vodka! Tasteless and colourless — of course!

ANGELA: Why don't you try and find out if some was missing,

just to put your mind at rest?

ELLEN: Someone could have given it to her, someone who hated her.

ANGELA: Ellen! For goodness sake, I'm supposed to be the one with the vivid imagination! No one gave it to her, she took it herself.

ELLEN: But was it for her? Or for me? *(she picks up flask)*

ANGELA: Oh, for heaven's sake! *(she moves to door)*

ELLEN: Where are you going?

ANGELA: Out front. *(Phyllis enters)* Hallo Phyllis, how's it going?

PHYLLIS: Much better. Ruth seems so much more confident. Why don't you go and watch?

ANGELA: I will, and it will be a pleasure. I prefer my drama on the stage, behind the footlights, where it belongs. *(she exits)*

PHYLLIS: Thank you, Ellen, you kept your word.

ELLEN: But you didn't, did you?

PHYLLIS: What do you mean?

ELLEN: You said you'd tell me all you knew — but you didn't tell me everything.

PHYLLIS: I don't understand.

ELLEN: Oh, yes, Phyllis, you do. What happened to Hugh's vodka?

PHYLLIS: How did you find out?

ELLEN: That's what it was, wasn't it? Hugh's vodka . . . . how much did she have — a whole tumblerful neat?

PHYLLIS: It wasn't my fault, Ellen, I didn't mean —

ELLEN: No, you didn't mean it for her, did you? Pat was no danger, falling in love with the producer, that's an occupational hazard, isn't it? You weren't worried about that, but —

24

what about me? How do you feel when Hugh and I laugh together, sharing experiences, living over again a shared background and a shared understanding of the world we loved and left and still can't abandon, how do you feel about that, Phyllis? That's something real. It doesn't end with each production, because we're working together towards the next . . . . we have so much in common, Hugh and I, something you can never be part of.

PHYLLIS: Ellen — I've never seen you look like this — what's the matter? Why do you look at me like that?

ELLEN: Love and jealousy, the love Mary felt for Elizabeth, the jealousy for a younger woman, they've been part of our lives all these weeks, haven't they? And, not only on the stage. But they're dangerous emotions to play with, aren't they Phyllis? Once they get out of control, once they take over and force us to live out our own dramas, make our own tragedies, with the people we love and fear — what happens then, Phyllis? *What happens then?*

BETTY: *(runs on)* Water! Anyone got any drinking water?

PHYLLIS: What is it? What's happened? Is it Ruth?

BETTY: Ruth? She's fine, she's giving a wonderful performance, Hugh hasn't stopped her once, he's sitting there spellbound. It's the props, they say lightning never strikes in the same place, except in the theatre, of course, then it does.

PHYLLIS: Does what?

BETTY: Strikes twice. It's been spilt, all that raspberry cordial, all over the floor, just like last time. If only they'd put it in decent bottles —

ELLEN: You mean the wine we use in the play was spilt last time?

BETTY: That's right, only then it was me, just before Ruth was due to carry it on, but I managed — I found a bottle of water and topped it up and no one knew.

PHYLLIS: Where did you find that water?

BETTY: In your basket, but there's none there tonight, I looked.

Didn't you bring any?

PHYLLIS: No — we didn't bring any.

ELLEN: *(handing flask)* Here, use this, it's orange juice.

BETTY: Oh, thanks. We're nearly ready now, I'll give you a call. *(she exits)*

PHYLLIS: So you were right after all, it was the wine. She drank a whole goblet of almost neat vodka, Hugh's vodka, and I thought she'd stolen it. I never dreamed it was a mistake, only you, Ellen, you had such faith, you never faltered — and you were right all the time.

ELLEN: No, I was wrong, terribly wrong. Because I had faith in one person I suspected everyone else; because I was looking for malice and jealousy I found what I was looking for. Angela was right, drama is safer on the stage, behind the footlights.

PHYLLIS: What are you going to do now, Ellen?

ELLEN: Nothing. We know the truth now, and it's up to us to see that no one else does. This is our private tragedy, and it's got to end now, before someone else gets hurt. We're all involved in this, you and I and Hugh, we were the people who mattered to Pat, the people she cared about — she had no one else.

PHYLLIS: And Betty?

ELLEN: She mustn't carry the burden of regret and remorse all her life We're as much to blame as she is. You, for leaving that bottle unguarded, Hugh, for his attack on Pat, and I for leaving her when she wasn't fit to be left. We've worked together so often in the past to put a Show on, now we must work to keep this to ourselves. We can't alter the past, but we can affect the future of Betty and the Society too. It's up to us to do it.

BETTY. *(Betty's voice is heard faintly and approaching)* Curtain going up, beginners please, beginners please!

PHYLLIS: I must go, good luck, Ellen. *(she moves to door as*

Betty enters)

BETTY: Hugh's yelling for you, Phyllis.

PHYLLIS: I'm going. *(she exits)*

BETTY: Are you ready, Ellen?

ELLEN: Yes, I'm ready . . . . What's the matter, Betty,, you look absolutely terrified

BETTY: I am terrified — look — I'm shaking like a leaf.

ELLEN: *(laughing)* Oh, that's nothing, you're just suffering from stage fright.

BETTY: Nothing! But it's a terrible feeling, absolutely terrible! If I'm like this at a dress rehearsal what shall I be like on the night?

ELLEN: You'll be fine, Betty, just fine. It's going to be a great occasion for you, your very first part. Come on, we'll go on together, the stage is waiting, and you've nothing to worry about, I promise you. Nothing to worry about at all.

They exit as

THE CURTAIN FALLS